What's it like to live in ...?

Italy

by Jillian Powell

WAYLAND

Other titles in the What's it like to live in? series:
Canada   France   Jamaica

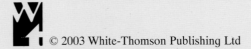 © 2003 White-Thomson Publishing Ltd

Produced for Hodder Wayland by
White-Thomson Publishing
2/3 St Andrew's Place, Lewes, East Sussex BN7 1UP

Published in Great Britain in 2003 by Hodder Wayland, an
imprint of Hodder Children's Books.
Reprinted in 2004

This paperback edition published in 2007 by Wayland,
an imprint of Hachette Children's Books

Editor: Sarah Doughty
Designer: Tim Mayer
Consultant: Lorraine Harrison
Language consultant: Norah Granger – Former head teacher
and senior lecturer in Early Years Education at the
University of Brighton
Picture research: Shelley Noronha – Glass Onion Pictures

The right of Jillian Powell to be identified as the author of
this Work has been asserted by her in accordance with the
Copyright, Designs and Patents Act 1988.

British Library Cataloguing in Publication Data
  Powell, Jillian
  What's it like to live in Italy?
  1. Italy - Social life and customs - Juvenile literature
  I. Title II. Doughty, Sarah
  945
ISBN-13: 978 0 7502 5118 1

Printed and bound in China

Hachette Children's Books
338 Euston Road, London NW1 3BH

Picture acknowledgements
Cephas (Don McKinnell) 16; Corbis 4, 24; Eye Ubiquitous
(Chris Fairclough) 3; HWPL (Chris Fairclough) 18, 21, 23;
Impact (Brian Harris) 8; Greg Evans Picture Library 11, 17;
Hulton Getty 20 (Image Bank), 22 (Tony Stone), 25 (All
Sport); Hutchison Library (K. Rogers) 27; James Davis
Travel 9; Robert Harding Picture Library Ltd/Alamy cover;
Topham Picturepoint 7, 19, 26; WTPix (Chris Fairclough) 6,
10, 12, 13, 15, 28 (centre).

Every effort has been made to trace copyright holders.
However, the publishers apologize for any unintentional
omissions and would be pleased in such cases to add an
acknowledgement in any future editions.

Contents

Where is Italy?

Italy is in the **Mediterranean region** of southern Europe. It is a long country, shaped like a boot, bordered mainly by the sea.

In Rome many tourists come to see the Trevi fountain.

Nearly 58 million people live in Italy. Its capital is Rome. Italy is a popular place for tourists to visit.

Italy's place in the world

ITALY FACTS

Italy stretches 1,200 km from north to south.

Sicily and Sardinia are the largest Italian islands.

The largest cities are Rome, Milan, Naples and Turin.

SWITZERLAND

AUSTRIA

SLOVENIA

FRANCE

Alps

Dolomites

Trieste

Milan

Lake Garda

Venice

Turin

Po

Genoa

Pisa

Arno

Florence

Siena

Tiber

ITALY

Apennines

Pescara

Rome

ADRIATIC SEA

Bari

Naples

Brindisi

0   100 kilometres

0   100 miles

N
W   E
S

Sardinia

Calgari

Messina

Palermo

Sicily

Siracuse

MEDITERRANEAN SEA

5

Cities

Many cities in Italy, such as Rome, Florence and Pisa started as **settlements** along the banks of a river. Often the oldest part of a city is by a river.

The city of Pisa on the River Arno.

Today nearly three million people live in Rome. Most live in the **suburbs** of the city but go into the centre to work or to visit the shops.

Rome's streets are often busy with people.

The landscape

Italy has some high mountains, such as the Alps. It also has vast areas of gentle hills and a wide area of flat **plains**.

The region of Tuscany has a landscape of gently sloping hills.

Lake Garda is
the largest of
the Italian lakes.

▶

Italy has many beautiful lakes.
It also has 7,600 km of coastline.
Italy's lakes and coastal areas
are very popular with visitors.

The weather

Most of Italy has hot, dry summers and mild winters. This is called a Mediterranean **climate**. The south is hot and dry for most of the year.

Italy is warm and sunny in summer.

In winter skiers enjoy deep snow in the Italian Alps.

In the mountains of the north, summers are short and the winters are cold with snow. Spring and autumn can be rainy.

Transport

People travel around Italy in cars, buses and trains. Motor scooters are a popular means of transport.

A scooter is a fast way of getting around town.

Ships and boats visit busy ports and harbours such as Venice, Genoa and Naples. Rome and Milan have trams and underground trains.

Big cities have electric trams as well as buses.

Farming

Almost a third of Italy's land is used for farming. In the south, farmers grow fruit and vegetables including grapes and olives.

Italy's sunny climate is ideal for growing grapes to make wine.

On the plains, some farmers grow grass for hay. Others grow wheat as a **cereal** and use the stalks for **straw**. In the hills, some farmers keep sheep and goats.

A tractor pulling the machinery that bundles up straw.

Food

Italians love cooking at home or eating out. Pizza and pasta are favourite Italian foods. There are around 400 different types of pasta!

A chef throws pizza dough up in the air to stretch and shape it.

Some regions of Italy are famous for certain foods. Naples is known for its seafood and its ice cream.

Ice cream is a popular treat in Italy and there are many flavours.

Shopping

Italy has all kinds of shops, from large supermarkets to small shops. There are market stalls that sell only bread or cakes, or fruit and vegetables.

Italy has colourful open-air markets.

The big cities have smart shops that sell designer clothes and other fashion goods.

The Italian designer, Gucci, is famous for shoes and handbags.

Houses and homes

In Italian cities, many people live in flats in the suburbs. Some homes have balconies where people can sit outside in the sunshine.

These Italian homes are mainly flats.

In the countryside, more people live in houses than flats. Many homes are built from local stone with clay tiled roofs.

These houses are in the countryside, near Lake Garda.

At work

Italy has many kinds of **industry**, especially in the north. Factories **process** foods, and make cars, machinery, chemicals, clothing and **textiles**.

Cars are built in factories and sold all over the world.

Tourism is a very important industry because it **employs** people all over Italy. There are also many new jobs in **technology**.

Many tourists come to Italy for its climate and to see its beautiful old buildings.

Having fun

Football, cycling and ball games are popular in Italy. Other activities include going to the cinema or visiting **Internet cafés**.

Children enjoy a game of football on a playing field.

Italians also enjoy watching sports such as **Grand Prix** motor racing. Many Italians look forward to the Giro d'Italia, a cycle race that tours Italy every spring.

The Grand Prix takes place near Milan every year.

Festivals

In Italy, there are exciting **festivals** all through the year. Crowds of people come to take part or watch. Many wear colourful costumes.

People wear colourful masks for the festival in Venice in February.

The streets are filled with **processions** or races at festival time. Some celebrate Saints' days. Others celebrate seasonal foods such as mushrooms found in the woods in autumn.

The Palio is a famous horse-race held in Siena in the summer.

Italian scrapbook

This is a scrapbook of some everyday things you might find in Italy.

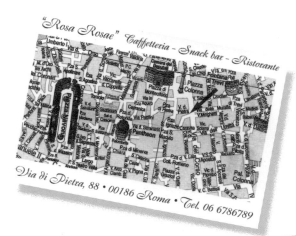

A card to show where to find a restaurant in Rome.

This is a postcard of the Rialto Bridge, in Venice.

Italians use euros. These can be spent in many countries in Europe.

A ticket to enter a church museum.

A bus and train ticket.

Glossary

Cereal A crop such as wheat, grown for food.

Climate The types of weather that usually happen in one place.

Employ To give people work to do to earn a living.

Festivals Times of celebration.

Grand Prix A yearly event of fast cars racing around a track.

Industry Work that employs lots of people, often in factories.

Internet cafés Places where people can meet, use the Internet and send e-mails.

Mediterranean The areas that border the Mediterranean Sea.

Plains Large areas of flat ground.

Process To change something so it is ready for use.

Processions Crowds of people walking as part of a festival or ceremony.

Region A part of a country.

Settlements Places where people have built houses.

Straw Dry cut stalks of grain, used as bedding for animals.

Suburbs Areas on the edges of a city where people live.

Technology Work to do with computers or machinery.

Textiles Materials used for clothes and furnishings.

Tourism Work to do with visitors and holidaymakers.

Further information

Some Italian words

cappuccino	milky coffee
carnevale	carnival
chiesa	church
gelato	ice cream
grazie	thank you
ferie	feast days/holidays
panetteria	bread shop
per favore	please
piazza	town square
posta	post office
ristorante/trattoria	restaurant

Books to read

Festivals and Food Italy by Saviour Pirotta (Wayland, 2006)
Italy by Fiona Tankard (Cherrytree, 2002)
Next Stop Italy by Fred Martin (Heinemann Children's Library, 1998)
Rome by Nicola Barber (Evans Brothers, 2003)
Step into Italy by Clare Boast (Heinemann Children's Library, 1998)

Index